James Wolfe and Quebec House

Kent

THE NATIONAL TRUST

Death and Glory

This medal was issued by John Kirk to commemorate Wolfe's conquest of Quebec. It is based on a wax relief modelled by the sculptor Isaac Gosset. Wolfe is shown wearing Antique armour, as in Wilton's bust (see p.6)

On 2 January 1727 Henrietta Wolfe gave birth to her first son, James, at Westerham vicarage, where she was staying while her husband Edward was away with his regiment. The previous year the family had taken up residence down the hill at Quebec House (then known as Spiers). Here James Wolfe spent his first eleven years, before the family moved to Greenwich. In 1741, at the age of fourteen, he was commissioned into his father's regiment of Marines, and for the rest of his life he led the nomadic existence of an army officer.

Wolfe's brief career reached its dramatic climax on the Heights of Abraham, which he scaled stealthily in September 1759 to confront a startled French army under Montcalm on the plain before Quebec. The battle that followed effectively decided the future of North America. Wolfe died at the moment of victory and, like Nelson after Trafalgar, instantly became a national hero. His triumphant victory and poignant death were commemorated in statues and songs, paintings and prints, many of which have now found their way to Quebec House. Over the years the house itself has undergone several structural changes (see p.4), but today its main features appear much the same as when the Wolfe family lived here.

The Death of Wolfe; coloured mezzotint after Edward Penny's 1763 painting, which was the most accurate contemporary depiction of the event

(*Opposite*) *Wolfe at Quebec*; detail of a version of J.S.C. Schaak's 1762 painting, which hangs in the Bicentenary Room. Wolfe wears a black armband, because he was in mourning for his father

The 18th-century cutlery in the Bicentenary Room once belonged to the Wolfe family

Quebec House

The plaque beside the front door commemorates Joseph Bowles Learmont, who gave Quebec House to the National Trust

The niches in the walls of the stables were designed to hold bee skeps (traditional hives made from woven straw)

(*Right*) A 19th-century view of Quebec House, before the gables were restored (David and Catherine Boston collection)

(*Opposite*) The front entrance

The present house, built of brick and Kent ragstone, is almost square, with no fewer than twelve gables, three on each façade. Originally it was smaller and less regular: in the internal north wall of the Parlour one can see how a Tudor mullioned window had to be blocked up when the main staircase was added during the 17th century. Another was found in 1968 during treatment for death-watch beetle; it can be seen in the album of photographs in the Bicentenary Room. The stable building, at the rear of the walled garden, also dates from Tudor times.

In view of the comparatively short time that the Wolfes were at Spiers, it is improbable that the family made any important alterations to the house. Later in the 18th century, or early in the 19th, extensive changes took place, including the complete remodelling of the south front to give it a plain square appearance, without gables, presumably to conform with current fashion. In the early 20th century, the south front was reconstructed once again on the lines of the 17th-century plan, and the three missing gables were replaced.

Later Owners

Not much is known about who lived here between the time the Wolfes moved to Greenwich in 1738 and the 20th century. In 1792 John Hemming granted a 1,000-year lease to the estate of John Saunders, one of whose family, William Saunders, occupied the house in the early 19th century. The building was divided into two dwellings – Quebec House East and West – by 1849, when John Howard, a miller, acquired the lease to the former. He may well have operated the mill which used to stand at the end of Mill Street close by Quebec House. Howard went bankrupt, but his family continued to occupy Quebec House East until 1900, when Colonel Charles Warde of Squerryes Court acquired the leasehold of the whole house.

Quebec House West was a 'Commercial School' run by Charles Carreck until 1884–5. From then until 1900 it was the home of Dr J.R. Russell, after whom the building housing Westerham's modern medical centre and Council Chambers is named. Colonel Warde set about an extensive renovation of the house, including the restoration of the gables to the front façade.

The Wolfe connection aroused the interest of Joseph Bowles Learmont of Montreal, who was seeking a suitable property to serve as a permanent memorial to Wolfe and his historical connection with Canada. In 1913 he bought Quebec House from the executors of Colonel Warde (who had died in 1912), but unfortunately he himself died in 1914. However, he had made his intentions clear in his will, and his widow presented the house to the National Trust in 1918. It was one of the first historic buildings to be acquired by the Trust.

Tour of the House

A bronze cast of Joseph Wilton's bust of Wolfe (Parlour). Wilton also designed Wolfe's tomb in Westminster Abbey (illustrated on p.16)

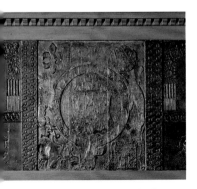

The overmantel in the Parlour is carved with the much-mutilated coat of arms of Henry VII

(*Opposite*) A Royal Lancashire Militia infantryman with a flintlock musket similar to that on show in the Entrance Hall; watercolour by Edward Dayes (Entrance Hall)

The Entrance Hall

Much of the panelling dates from the 17th century, but it has since been considerably patched. The Tudor fireplace contains a most appropriate cast-iron fireback, decorated with the French fleur-de-lis, which appears on the flag of Quebec.

The set of nine watercolours by Edward Dayes illustrates the uniforms and arms drill of the Lancashire Militia in the late 18th century. Above the fireplace hang watercolour portraits of Mr and Mrs Learmont, painted in 1911 by B.M.L. Huntington. They were presented to Quebec House in 1973 by Mrs Charles Stuart McEuan, a niece of Mrs Learmont.

The furniture includes an 18th-century Flemish oak buffet and the pair of Charles II walnut side-chairs, with richly carved frames and caned seats. Above the fireplace hangs a flintlock musket of 1758. This was the standard firearm of the infantry soldier during the Quebec campaign. The halberd in the corner was carried by a sergeant, more as a badge of rank than a weapon.

The Parlour

This room lies off the Hall to the left. The 17th-century pine panelling has been given a decorative graining similar to that discovered under ten layers of paint, which may date from the Wolfes' time. Above the fireplace is a coarsely carved early 17th-century overmantel, in which the much-mutilated arms of Henry VII were inserted.

The room is dominated by a bronze bust of Wolfe, *c*.1760, by Joseph Wilton, who sculpted his monument in Westminster Abbey. He is shown in classical dress, with the rather nice touch of epaulettes in the shape of wolf heads.

Unfortunately, decay prevented Wilton from taking a death-mask of Wolfe's face, nor were there any lifetime portraits of him as a grown man. However, a servant who bore a striking resemblance to Wolfe served as a model, with help from Lord Edgcumbe, who corrected the finer details from memory.

Wolfe dies many times at Quebec House. The most accurate representation is the coloured mezzotint of 1779 after Edward Penny's painting of 1764. It shows Wolfe being attended by an officer and two grenadiers. Most impressive is George Roth Junior's 1784 copy of Benjamin West's *Death of Wolfe* of 1770, which marked a turning point in historical portraiture. Previously, dead heroes had been depicted in classical dress (as in Wilton's bust). West chose to portray Wolfe and the attendant throng in the uniform of the day. The result was an immense success, which became, through West's numerous painted versions and William Woollett's engraving, one of the most famous images of the 18th century. Some of the actual artefacts shown in the painting were discovered in 1992 and are now in the British Museum.

West's approach was closely followed by Watteau de Lille in his *Death of Montcalm*, of which a coloured engraving hangs on the fireplace wall. It is even more inaccurate, as the French commander did not die on the battlefield, but the following day in Quebec's Ursuline Convent.

In the glazed corner cabinet is displayed part of the Quebec House collection of Wolfe memorabilia. Many were the personal possessions of James's mother, Henrietta Wolfe.

The Bow figurine
of Wolfe in the
Bicentenary Room
is based on Schaak's
painting (illustrated
on p.3)

The travelling canteen
used by Wolfe during the
Quebec campaign

The Inner Hall

There is a good opportunity here to compare the engravings of the deaths of Wolfe and Montcalm, which hang each side of the small 17th-century oak door. This leads to the cellars which run underneath parts of the house, but which are not open to view.

Among the varied presentations of Wolfe, an attractive portrayal is the coloured sketch by George Townshend, one of Wolfe's brigadiers; a photograph of it can be seen on the left-hand wall as one steps from the Hall into the Inner Hall. The original is in the McCord Museum, McGill University, Montreal. It is dated 1759, but was probably executed from memory after Wolfe's death as a memento for the general's friend and Adjutant-General, Isaac Barré. This flattering image is in marked contrast to the caricatures of Wolfe that Townshend had produced during his lifetime. Above the door is a version – possibly by the artist, J.S.C. Schaak, himself – of one of the most popular posthumous images of Wolfe, his right arm outstretched, with the storming of the Heights of Abraham behind.

The Bicentenary Room

In the Wolfes' time this must have been one of the main rooms, but in the 19th century it was subdivided into four and used as servants' quarters. Fortunately, its panelling, which dates from about 1680, was not removed. In 1959, thanks mainly to the generosity of Canadians on both sides of the Atlantic, it was possible to

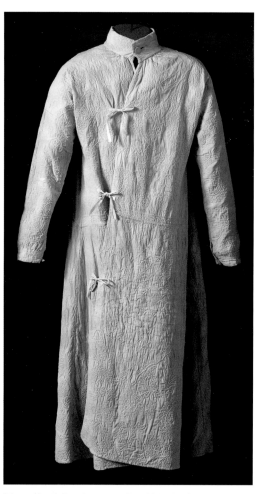

The quilted dressing gown in which Wolfe is said to have been wrapped shortly before his burial (Bicentenary Room)

commemorate the bicentenary of the death of Wolfe and the capture of Quebec by restoring it to its former state.

One of the most important pieces of evidence for Wolfe's appearance is the pencil profile that can be seen to the left of the fireplace. This sketch appears entirely spontaneous and indeed is thought to have been drawn from life by Wolfe's principal aide-de-camp, Captain Hervey Smyth, on a page torn from a field notebook shortly before the battle. It is close to being a caricature, emphasising Wolfe's distinctive features of sloping forehead, pointed nose and receding chin. The drawing influenced the many posthumous portraits of Wolfe, such as the full-length oil, after Schaak, which hangs at the other end of the room.

Shades of Benjamin West appear twice more in the form of a mid-19th-century Pontypool-ware tray, above the fireplace, and a very fragile early 19th-century version of *The Death of Wolfe*, embroidered in coloured silks, between the windows. On the wall above the 17th-century oak chest are portraits of Wolfe's parents, Edward and Henrietta.

Behind the door are the Wolfe family bible and family tree, originally prepared in 1963 by the Garter King of Arms and extended in 1986 by courtesy of the Wolfe Society. On the back is another tree showing Wolfe's descent through his mother's side from Edward III and Hotspur.

By the door is a piece of furniture that strongly evokes the comfort in which an 18th-century general officer contrived to live even on active service. This is the travelling canteen made for Wolfe's use during the Quebec campaign. Some of the original contents are in the showcase nearby, including griddle, frying pan, canisters, cruet and glass decanters. The case also contains part of a set of 18th-century cutlery formerly in the possession of the Wolfe family.

In the cabinets at the other end of the room are Wolfe's quilted cotton dressing-gown, in which his body was wrapped immediately before it was buried, and his powder cloak. The latter was worn to protect the clothing, while the hair and wig was being powdered. Both were probably made in Flanders. Above the cloak is a miniature portrait of Wolfe as a young man, which was copied about 1820 from an oil painting at Squerryes, painted from life about 1741. To the right is the telescope lent to Wolfe by Colonel Williamson, who commanded the Royal Artillery at Quebec.

Captain Hervey Smyth's sketch of Wolfe's distinctive profile is one of the few lifetime likenesses of him

(*Below*) The Bicentenary Room

The Capture of Louisbourg, by Richard Paton (Drawing Room)

The Drawing Room

The Staircase and Landings

The wide mid-17th-century staircase ascends to the full height of the house. On the walls is hung a series of engravings by a variety of different engravers, published in 1761 and based on original 'drawings on the spot' by Richard Short. Several show the extensive damage caused by the British bombardment during the siege of Quebec.

On the half-landing is Richard Houston's 1766–7 mezzotint based on the Schaak portrait of *Wolfe at Quebec*. Beside it is a pirated copy (reversed in printing) by the unscrupulous printseller Richard Purcell, who used the pseudonym Corbut. They reflect the ready market for images of Wolfe immediately after his death.

Continuing up the stairs towards the second-floor half-landing, you will find

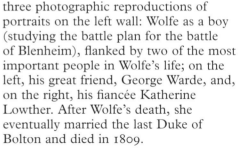

three photographic reproductions of portraits on the left wall: Wolfe as a boy (studying the battle plan for the battle of Blenheim), flanked by two of the most important people in Wolfe's life; on the left, his great friend, George Warde, and, on the right, his fiancée Katherine Lowther. After Wolfe's death, she eventually married the last Duke of Bolton and died in 1809.

The Drawing Room

This large panelled room overlooking the front garden and the street beyond was split into two rooms, probably when the house itself was divided into East and West. It was restored to its original appearance during the extensive alterations carried out by Colonel Warde after 1900.

None of the furniture has any connection with the Wolfe family, but has been chosen for its appropriateness to the house. The best pieces are: an early 18th-century oak tallboy (behind the door), a large Queen Anne walnut chest-of-drawers with a brushing slide, and also a bureau of the same period, which has suffered much later alteration.

In the corner next to the panelled door is an attractive late 17th-century longcase clock. The movement is by the well-known London clockmaker Edmund Aplee (more commonly spelt Appley) of Charing Cross, whose name is engraved on the dial. The walnut case, inlaid with marquetry, is contemporary with the movement, though the base is a later addition.

By the clock is a mellow mahogany square piano, made in 1788 by the first John Broadwood, who went into partnership with the Swiss-born

harpsichord maker Burkat Shudi in 1770, having married Shudi's daughter. Shudi retired soon afterwards, and John Broadwood assumed control in 1783.

On the piano is a framed piece of 18th-century music entitled 'Britannia or the Death of Wolfe', whose words reflect the sentimentality of the age. They were written by the author of *The Rights of Man*, Thomas Paine, while he was living in Lewes between 1768 and 1774. He became editor of the *Pennsylvania Magazine*, in which he published the song in March 1775, commenting to the publishers that 'I have not pursued the worn out tract of modern song but have thrown it into fable'.

The prints and painting are, with one exception, associated with Wolfe and Canada, ranging from a grisaille copy of West's *Death of Wolfe* to coloured engravings of Montreal (left of fireplace) and lithographs of Quebec (right of fireplace). The most impressive painting is that above the bureau, by Richard Paton, depicting the capture of Louisbourg in 1758, in which Wolfe played such a prominent part (see p.14). The painting above the fireplace was originally also thought to be of Louisbourg, but it is in fact of the Battle of Sole Bay in 1672, after Van der Velde's picture in the National Maritime Museum.

The panel of *toile de Jouy* printed cotton on the Staircase is based on Benjamin West's famous painting

James Wolfe's Early Years

James Wolfe aged fourteen. This miniature in the Bicentenary Room was probably based on a portrait at nearby Squerryes Court, the home of the Warde family, who were friends of the Wolfes

Wolfe came from a military family. His father, Edward, fought in Flanders under Marlborough and was a lieutenant-colonel by the age of 32. Seven years later, in 1724, he married Henrietta Thompson, the daughter of a Yorkshire squire; she was twenty years his junior. In 1726 they moved from York to Westerham, where they rented the house (then called Spiers) which is now known as Quebec House. On 2 January 1727 Mrs Wolfe gave birth to her elder son, James, at Westerham vicarage, a little way up the hill and on the opposite side of the road from Spiers, where she was staying during the absence of her husband with his regiment. A year later her second son, Edward, was born at Spiers itself. (He was to die on active service in Flanders aged sixteen.) The Wolfe family continued to live there until they moved to Greenwich in 1738 – that is, until James was eleven years old.

Wolfe entered the family profession young and rose fast. In 1741, at the age of fourteen, he was given his first commission as second lieutenant in his father's regiment of Marines. Early in the following year he obtained a transfer to the 12th Regiment of Foot and was acting adjutant of that regiment two years later at the Battle of Dettingen, at which the King, George II, was present, the last such occasion in British history. In a letter home to his father, Wolfe gave a vivid account of the battle, during which his own horse was shot from under him so that he was 'obliged to do the duty of an adjutant all that and the next day on foot, in a pair of heavy boots'.

In 1745 he was already a brigade-major, and was sent with the army under General Wade to oppose Bonnie Prince Charlie in his advance from the north and was present at Culloden. In 1747 he was again in the Netherlands, and in the same year began a four-year-long and ultimately fruitless courtship of Elizabeth Lawson. The match was opposed by Wolfe's mother, to whom he wrote after Elizabeth had rejected him:

There is a great probability I shall never marry. I shall hardly engage in an affair of that nature purely for the money, nor do I believe that my infatuation will ever be strong enough to persuade me that people cannot live without it.

Henrietta Wolfe (1704–64); portrait in the Bicentenary Room

Wolfe was not an easy man, but then few great commanders are. 'My temper is much too warm,' he later admitted to his mother, 'and sudden resentment forces out expressions and even actions that are neither justifiable nor excusable.' His temper was not improved by chronic rheumatism and consumption, which his mother's grisly patent cures only worsened. He was tall and painfully thin, with a pointed nose and receding chin, pale blue eyes, long awkward fingers and bright red hair, which he frequently wore long and loose without the traditional powdered military wig. He had few of the social graces ('I can neither laugh nor sing, nor talk an hour upon nothing'), but all agreed that he had a 'peculiar turn for war'.

Wolfe was acknowledged as a brilliant trainer of infantry and his *Instructions to Young Officers* was highly regarded. Although he took a traditionally dim view of the men he commanded, he won their loyalty and obedience in action by his concern for their welfare. In 1750, when still only 23 years old, he was promoted to a lieutenant-colonelcy in Scotland and, in an effort to improve his education and acquire the social accomplishments essential for promotion to senior military command, applied much of his leisure to mathematics, Latin, French, and dancing.

Wolfe's chance came with the outbreak in 1756 of the Seven Years War against France. In 1757 the Prime Minister, William Pitt the Elder, sanctioned a series of raids against the French coast in support of Britain's ally in the east, the Prussian King, Frederick the Great. Wolfe joined a force commanded by Elizabeth Lawson's uncle, General Mordaunt, which was

chosen to attack Rochefort. Under heavy fire he successfully got a landing party ashore, but, because of dithering among the senior commanders, 'the lucky moment in war', as he called it, was lost and the attack petered out in humiliating failure. 'We blundered most egregiously on all sides – sea and land', he wrote later. However, Wolfe's zeal in this, the first of his three combined operations, brought him special commendation from George II, who promoted him to full colonel, and is later said to have remarked, 'Mad is he? Then I hope he will bite some other of my generals.'

Wolfe had a reputation as a brilliant trainer of infantry

General Edward Wolfe (1685–1759); portrait in the Bicentenary Room

Wolfe at Quebec

The Marquis de Montcalm, who commanded the French forces at Quebec

Wolfe hunts for French spies in the army latrines. This caricature by his difficult, but gifted, subordinate George Townshend satirises Wolfe's concern for both security and hygiene (McCord Museum, McGill University)

In 1758 Wolfe was sent in command of a brigade in General Amherst's Canadian expedition against the French fortress of Louisbourg on Cape Breton Island, which occupied a vital strategic position commanding the southern approaches to the St Lawrence River, the principal supply route for Quebec, Montreal and the lands of 'New France'. Wolfe effected his famous landing at Freshwater Cove, successfully storming a position strongly held by the French. In less than a month Louisbourg surrendered. In the spring of 1759, still only 32, Wolfe was chosen by Pitt to command the force to be sent up the St Lawrence against Quebec, while Amherst advanced north on Montreal by the inland route, and a third force under General Prideaux marched on Niagara.

The last month of Wolfe's life is part of British history. By the end of June he had established his army at Point Levy on the south bank of the St Lawrence. This enabled the fleet under the command of Admiral Saunders to move up into the basin of Quebec, and on 12 July the batteries near Point Levy began to bombard the town on the opposite bank. Wolfe ordered a frontal assault on the French army entrenched at the Beauport Lines to the east of Quebec, but it proved a bloody failure despite his cool leadership. 'I was no less than three times struck with splinters and had my stick knocked out of my hand with a cannonball', he told Saunders.

Wolfe's health, never robust, broke down completely through anxiety and over-exertion. 'You cannot cure my complaint,' he told his surgeon, 'but pray make me up so that I may be without pain for a few days, and be able to do my duty; that is all I want.' His condition obliged him to yield to the advice of his brigadiers, who opposed a second attack on the Beauport Lines, and it was finally agreed to revert to earlier plans to make a landing on the north bank above the town.

On the evening of the final assault, Wolfe's orders were read to the troops. Foreshadowing Nelson's famous signal at Trafalgar, he ended: 'The officers and men will remember what their country expects from them.' About midnight they embarked in small boats for the three-hour passage, slipping down-river with the turning tide. The weather was fine, the night calm, dark and still. They made the crossing in dead silence, bluffing their way through several challenges from French sentries, to land, as planned, at Anse au Foulon. Facing them were cliffs 175 feet high, but a path was found wide enough to take two men abreast. By dawn on 13 September Wolfe, with 4,500 men and two cannons, had occupied the Heights of Abraham on the plain to the west of Quebec.

When the news was brought to the incredulous Marquis de Montcalm, commanding the French forces, he decided at once to engage the British before they could dig in. The French advanced slowly at first against the British line. As they closed, discipline started to break down, the line became ragged and they began to fire prematurely. Wolfe's forces, instilled with his parade-ground discipline, waited until the enemy was only 40 yards away and then fired a single, stunning volley.

At that moment the outcome of the battle was effectively decided.

With typical disregard for his own safety, Wolfe placed himself in the thick of the fighting. Early in the engagement he was twice wounded, in the wrist and groin, before a third shot struck him mortally in the chest. Captain John Knox of the 43rd Regiment of Foot (Kennedy's) pieced together this account of Wolfe's last moments from the various versions:

… he desired those who were about him to lay him down; being asked if he would have a Surgeon he replied, 'it is needless; it is all over with me.' One of them cried out, 'they run, see how they run.' 'Who runs?' demanded our hero, with great earnestness, like a person roused from sleep. The Officer answered, 'The enemy, Sir; Egad, they give way everywhere.' Thereupon the General rejoined, 'Go one of you, my lads, to Colonel Burton – tell him to march Webb's regiment with all speed to Charles's River, to cut off the retreat of the fugitives from the bridge.' Then turning on his side he added, 'Now, God be praised, I will die in peace:' and thus expired.

Victory in battle, the one aim of his life, had been achieved.

Admiral Sir Charles Saunders, commander-in-chief of the British fleet on the St Lawrence River

On 13 September 1759 Wolfe's force scaled the Heights of Abraham in secret to confront a startled French army on the plain to the west of Quebec

Life after Death

Wolfe's death inspired numerous patriotic songs

Wolfe's body was brought back to Portsmouth on the *Royal William*, one of the ships of Admiral Saunders's fleet, which had done so much to assist the army in this superbly executed operation. He was buried in the Wolfe family vault in St Alphege church, Greenwich, on 20 November 1759, the same day that Admiral Hawke won the last of the three great victories of that 'Year of Victories': Minden, Quebec and Quiberon Bay.

But that was not the end of the story. Military commanders who die young at the moment of victory acquire a heroic aura that demands commemoration. Pitt gave a tearful encomium in the House of Commons, which was generally felt to be among the worst speeches of his career. His brother-in-law, Lord Temple, erected an obelisk in Wolfe's memory at Stowe in Buckinghamshire. The 3rd Duke of Richmond, who had served in 1753 in Wolfe's regiment, commissioned a bust from Joseph Wilton. A more grandiose monument, again by Wilton, followed in the English Valhalla, Westminster Abbey. Most famously, Benjamin West painted his *Death of Wolfe* in 1770, a dramatic mixture of quasi-authentic historical reconstruction and religious pathos.

In Wolfe's birthplace, Westerham, the more prominent memorials were to appear much later: the statue on the Green, unveiled by Field Marshall Lord Roberts in 1911, and the gift of Quebec House to the National Trust in 1918 as a permanent shrine to his memory. Initially, the tributes were more modest and were the inspiration of George Warde of Squerryes Court, who had been a close friend of Wolfe since childhood and was entrusted by Mrs Wolfe with the Wolfe family relics on her death in 1764. He erected a cenotaph in Squerryes park to mark the spot where Wolfe had received his first commission while visiting the Wardes. A group of Wolfe's friends also put up in Westerham church a marble tablet which incorporates a simple epitaph:

While George in sorrow bows his laurell'd head,
And bids the artist grace the soldier dead;
We raise no sculptur'd trophy to thy name,
Brave youth! the fairest in the list of fame.
Proud of thy birth, we boast th' auspicious year,
Struck with thy fall, we shed a general tear;
With humble grief inscribe one artless stone,
And from thy matchless honours date our own.

Joseph Wilton's Wolfe monument in Westminster Abbey